WHAT Am I?
Riddles for Kids

GAIL BOWLING

To order additional copies of this book, contact:
Xlibris
844-714-8691
www.Xlibris.com
Orders@Xlibris.com

ISBN: Softcover   978-1-6698-0020-0
         Hardcover   978-1-6698-0021-7
         EBook   978-1-6698-0019-4

Library of Congress Control Number: 2021923704

Print information available on the last page.

Rev. date: 10/26/2022

YOU EAT ME FOR A SPECIAL TREAT
I MELT AND DRIP SO PLEASE BE NEAT

ICE CREAM

I SPARKLE AND TWINKLE, I'M QUITE A DISH
AND I LIKE TO HEAR YOUR EVERY WISH

YOU CAN PLAY ME SITTING DOWN
MY KEY'S PRODUCE A PRETTY SOUND

YOU CAN PLANT AND WATCH ME GROW
BUT IF YOU DO YOU'LL HAVE TO MOW

YOU CAN LIVE WITHIN MY DOORS
SOMETIMES I'M BUILT WITH MANY FLOORS

HOUSE

I AM YELLOW AND SHINE REAL BRIGHT
I GO AWAY WHEN IT IS NIGHT

YOU CAN PUT ME ON YOUR FEET
OR IN THE CLOSET NICE AND NEAT

I HOLD TRASH AND SOMETIMES STINK
I'M OFTEN UNDER THE KITCHEN SINK

YOU CAN HANG ME ON THE WALL
SECURELY PLEASE OR I WILL FALL

I'M MOSTLY USED TO CUT OR PEEL
AND USUALLY MADE OF HARDENED STEEL

MY COLORS ARE BRIGHT SOME EVEN RED
I GROW OUTSIDE WITHIN A BED

YOU LOOK THRU ME FROM EITHER SIDE
CLOSE THE CURTAINS AND YOU CAN HIDE

YOU REST ON ME WHEN YOU NEED SLEEP
IF WIDE AWAKE JUST COUNT SOME SHEEP

I'M OUT AT NIGHT WHEN THE SUN IS DOWN
I SHINE REAL BRIGHT OVER EVERY TOWN

YOU WRITE WITH ME AND I CAN STAY
BUT DON'T ERASE, I'LL GO AWAY

I OPEN AND CLOSE AND OFTEN LOCK
TO COME THROUGH ME YOU
NEED TO KNOCK

SOMETIMES I'M SHORT OR I CAN BE TALL
IF YOU CLIMB MY LIMBS
PLEASE DON'T FALL

YOU CAN WEAR ME ON YOUR FACE AND SOMETIMES PUT ME IN A CASE

WHEN YOU BRUSH ME I WILL SHINE
BUT IF I KNOT THEN YOU WILL WHINE

I'M MOSTLY GROUNDED LIKE A DUD
BUT ADD SOME WATER AND I TURN TO MUD

Printed in the United States
by Baker & Taylor Publisher Services